A JUNIOR RANGER'S GUIDE TO THE NATIONAL PARKS

Reviews of Parks Visited from 2015 through 2020

ERIC FEICHTHALER, JR.

ISBN-13: 9798649170321

Cover design by: Eric Feichthaler, Jr.

Library of Congress Control Number: 2018675309

Printed in the United States of America

DEDICATION

I dedicate this book to all the park rangers who devote themselves to promoting and protecting our nation's amazing national parks. I also want to thank my mom and dad for painstakingly planning every detail of our trips. I am so glad that Tyler, Emily, Lachlan, my parents and I could share these adventures together. It is exciting for me to now be in charge of most of the planning responsibilities for our upcoming trips to new parks none of us have ever visited – *Eric Feichthaler, Jr.*

Dear Fellow National Park Enthusiasts,

I hope you are as excited about visiting our country's national parks and monuments as I am. Our country is amazing and has so much for us to enjoy. Whenever I am on a trip to a new national park, I like to write about and draw what I see. I have been visiting national parks since I was 8 and have been documenting my travels in a journal with photos and memories. I have had the good fortune to travel to all 50 states in which I visited 48 national parks from 2015 – 2020. I have now visited 40 of our country's 62 parks and have visited several multiple times. Our national parks are an unparalleled place where hikers, photographers, nature lovers and families can have unique experiences which change with the time of day and time of year that you visit. I have included my overall rankings of the national parks based on their flora, fauna and natural characteristics like mountains. I hope you will enjoy reading about experiences and will have your own amazing experiences visiting these incredible treasures!

Sincerely,

Eric Feichthaler, Jr.

Table of Contents

National Park
Logbook

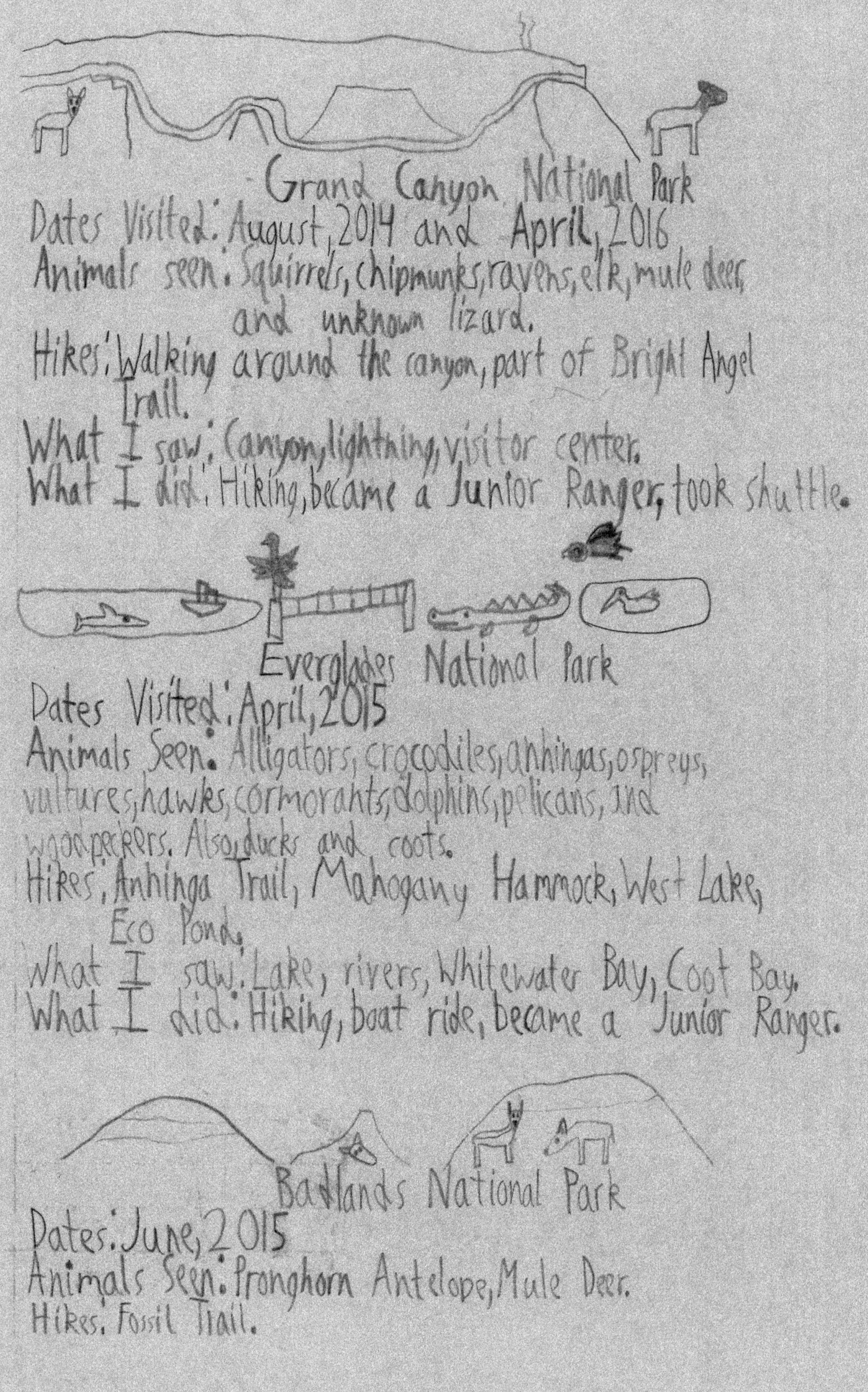

Grand Canyon National Park

Dates Visited: August, 2014 and April, 2016
Animals seen: Squirrels, chipmunks, ravens, elk, mule deer, and unknown lizard.
Hikes: Walking around the canyon, part of Bright Angel Trail.
What I saw: Canyon, lightning, visitor center.
What I did: Hiking, became a Junior Ranger, took shuttle.

Everglades National Park

Dates Visited: April, 2015
Animals Seen: Alligators, crocodiles, anhingas, ospreys, vultures, hawks, cormorants, dolphins, pelicans, and woodpeckers. Also, ducks and coots.
Hikes: Anhinga Trail, Mahogany Hammock, West Lake, Eco Pond.
What I saw: Lake, rivers, Whitewater Bay, Coot Bay.
What I did: Hiking, boat ride, became a Junior Ranger.

Badlands National Park

Dates: June, 2015
Animals Seen: Pronghorn Antelope, Mule Deer.
Hikes: Fossil Trail.

What I saw: Fossils of mammals, the Badlands.
What I did: Climbed small mountains, hiked, became a Junior
Ranger, took a scenic drive.

Yellowstone National Park

Dates Visited: June, 2015
Animals Seen: Bison, deer, pronghorn antelope, grizzly bears, black bears and cubs, elk, marmot, bighorn. Hikes: Upper Geyser Basin, Norris Geyser basin, Mammoth Hot Springs.
What I saw: Mountains, Mammoth Hot Springs, Norris Geyser Basin, Steamboat Geyser, Upper Geyser Basin, Old Faithful, Yellowstone Lake, Yellowstone River, Grand Canyon of the Yellowstone, 45th Parallel Bridge, Yellowstone National Park Museum.
What I did: Hiking, became a Junior Ranger, took Scenic Drive.

Yosemite National Park

Dates Visited: June, 2015
Animals Seen: Mule Deer, Coyote.
Hikes: Mariposa Grove, Lower Yosemite Falls.
What I saw: Sequoias, El Capitan, Half Dome, Yosemite Falls.
What I did: Hiked, took shuttle bus, became a Junior Ranger

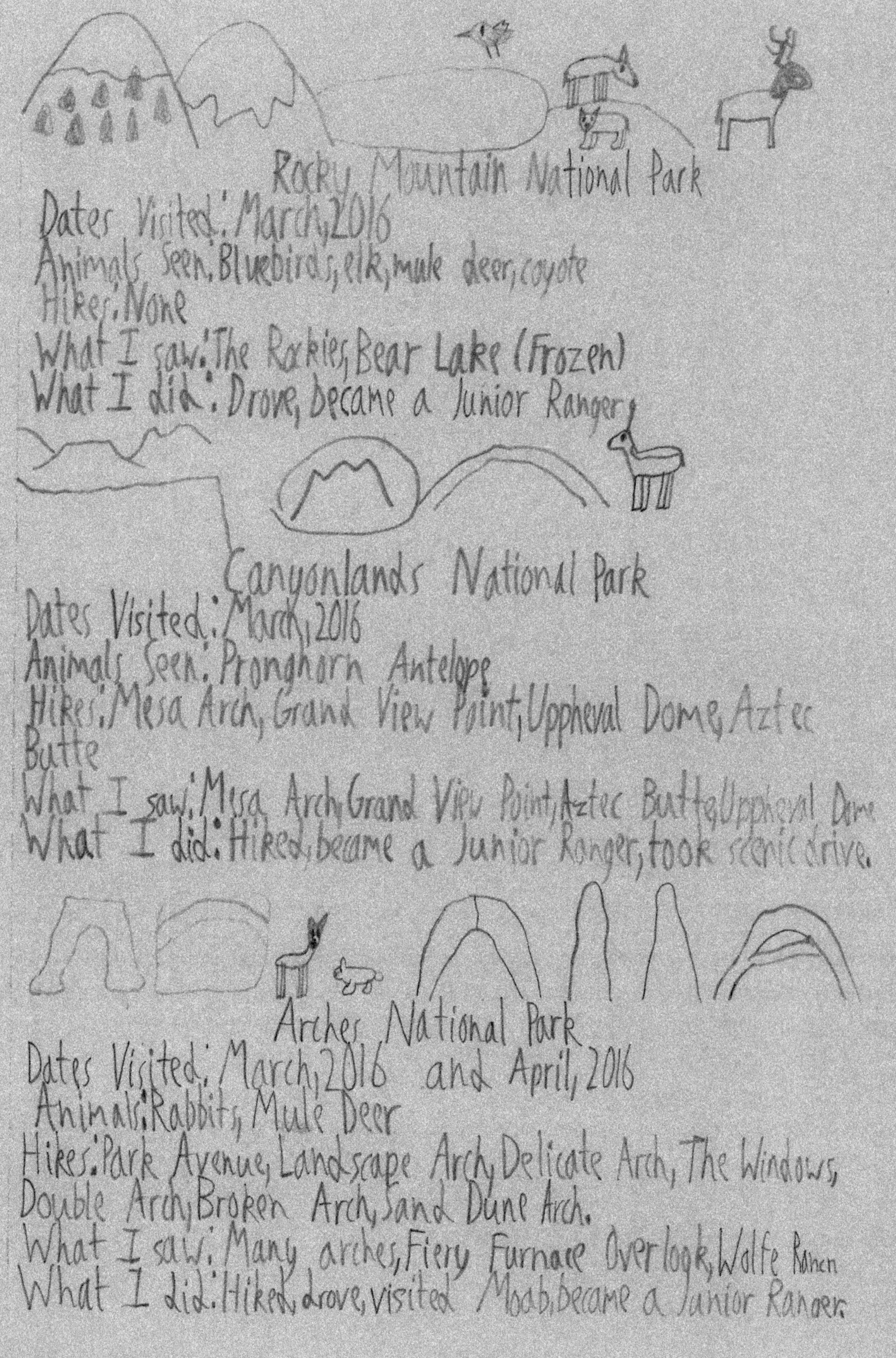

Rocky Mountain National Park

Dates Visited: March, 2016
Animals Seen: Bluebirds, elk, mule deer, coyote
Hikes: None
What I saw: The Rockies, Bear Lake (Frozen)
What I did: Drove, became a Junior Ranger.

Canyonlands National Park

Dates Visited: March, 2016
Animals Seen: Pronghorn Antelope
Hikes: Mesa Arch, Grand View Point, Uppheval Dome, Aztec Butte
What I saw: Mesa Arch, Grand View Point, Aztec Butte, Uppheval Dome
What I did: Hiked, became a Junior Ranger, took scenic drive.

Arches National Park

Dates Visited: March, 2016 and April, 2016
Animals: Rabbits, Mule Deer
Hikes: Park Avenue, Landscape Arch, Delicate Arch, The Windows, Double Arch, Broken Arch, Sand Dune Arch.
What I saw: Many arches, Fiery Furnace Overlook, Wolfe Ranch
What I did: Hiked, drove, visited Moab, became a Junior Ranger.

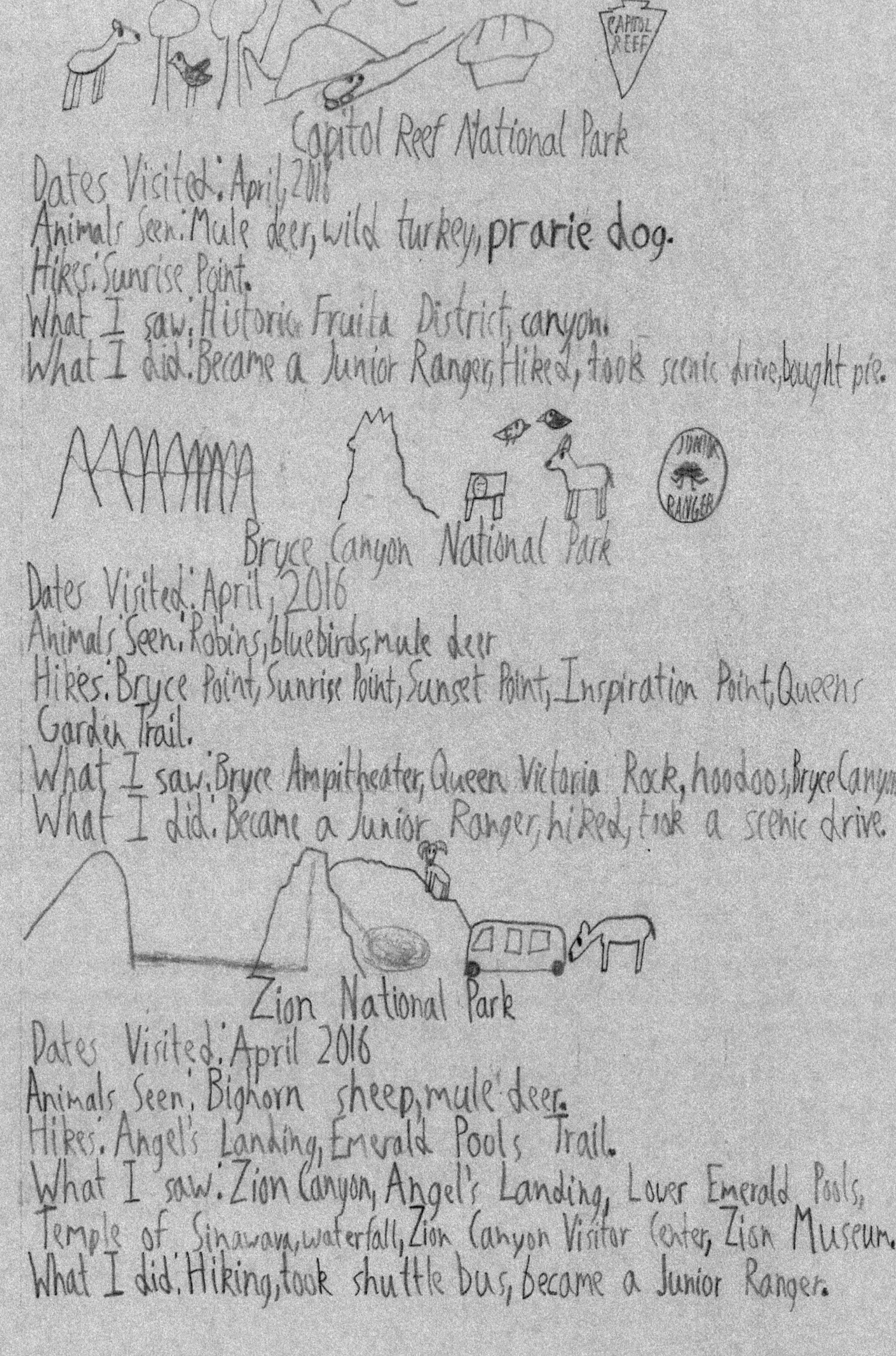

Capitol Reef National Park

Dates Visited: April, 2016
Animals Seen: Mule deer, wild turkey, prarie dog.
Hikes: Sunrise Point.
What I saw: Historic Fruita District, canyon.
What I did: Became a Junior Ranger, Hiked, took scenic drive, bought pie.

Bryce Canyon National Park

Dates Visited: April, 2016
Animals Seen: Robins, bluebirds, mule deer
Hikes: Bryce Point, Sunrise Point, Sunset Point, Inspiration Point, Queens Garden Trail.
What I saw: Bryce Ampitheater, Queen Victoria Rock, hoodoos, Bryce Canyon
What I did: Became a Junior Ranger, hiked, took a scenic drive.

Zion National Park

Dates Visited: April 2016
Animals Seen: Bighorn sheep, mule deer.
Hikes: Angel's Landing, Emerald Pools Trail.
What I saw: Zion Canyon, Angel's Landing, Lower Emerald Pools, Temple of Sinawava, waterfall, Zion Canyon Visitor Center, Zion Museum.
What I did: Hiking, took shuttle bus, became a Junior Ranger.

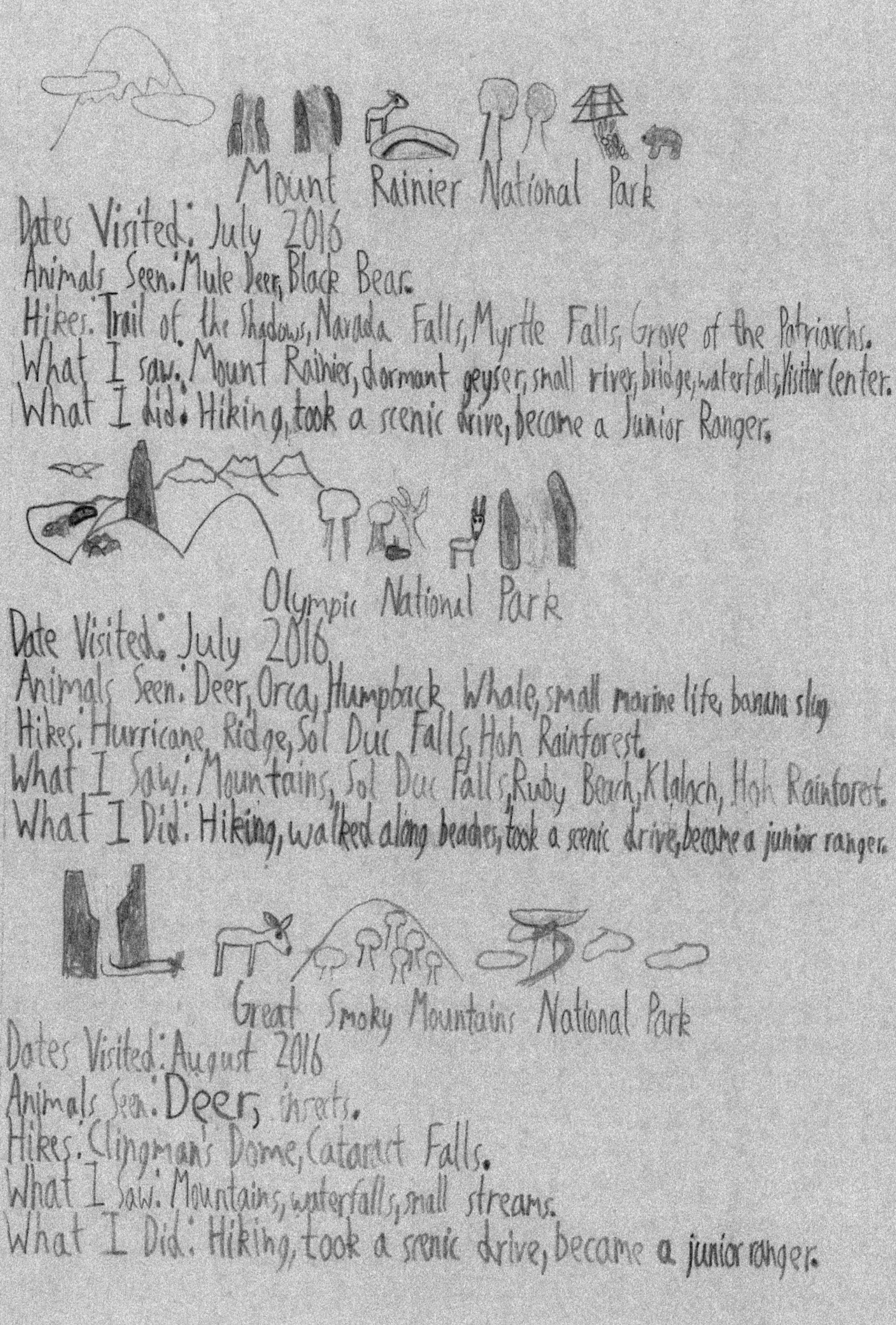

Mount Rainier National Park

Dates Visited: July 2016
Animals Seen: Mule Deer, Black Bear.
Hikes: Trail of the Shadows, Narada Falls, Myrtle Falls, Grove of the Patriarchs.
What I saw: Mount Rainier, dormant geyser, small river, bridge, waterfalls, visitor center.
What I did: Hiking, took a scenic drive, became a Junior Ranger.

Olympic National Park

Date Visited: July 2016
Animals Seen: Deer, Orca, Humpback Whale, small marine life, banana slug
Hikes: Hurricane Ridge, Sol Duc Falls, Hoh Rainforest.
What I Saw: Mountains, Sol Duc Falls, Ruby Beach, Klaloch, Hoh Rainforest.
What I Did: Hiking, walked along beaches, took a scenic drive, became a junior ranger.

Great Smoky Mountains National Park

Dates Visited: August 2016
Animals Seen: Deer, insects.
Hikes: Clingman's Dome, Cataract Falls.
What I Saw: Mountains, waterfalls, small streams.
What I Did: Hiking, took a scenic drive, became a junior ranger.

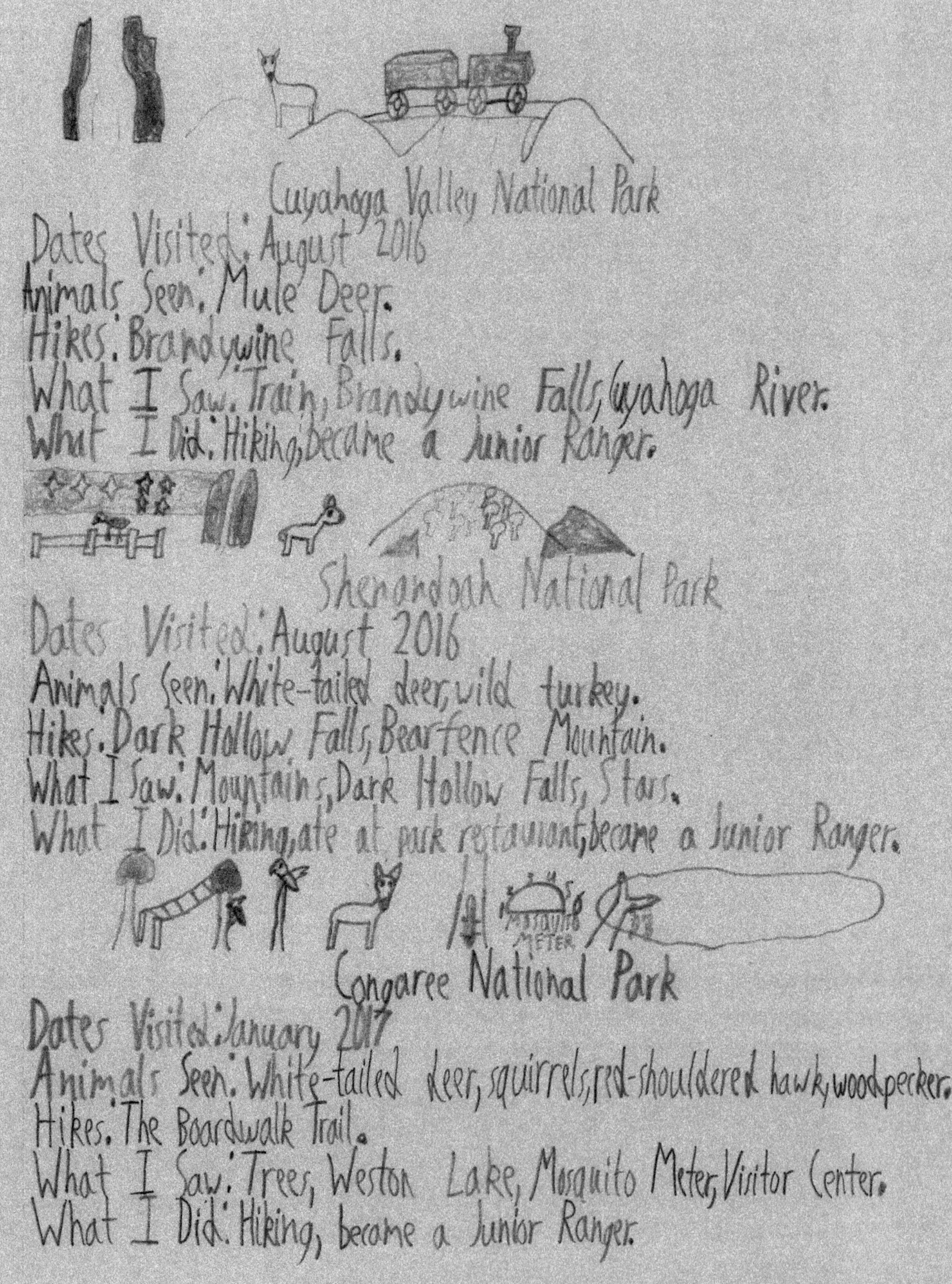

Cuyahoga Valley National Park

Dates Visited: August 2016
Animals Seen: Mule Deer.
Hikes: Brandywine Falls.
What I Saw: Train, Brandywine Falls, Cuyahoga River.
What I Did: Hiking, became a Junior Ranger.

Shenandoah National Park

Dates Visited: August 2016
Animals Seen: White-tailed deer, wild turkey.
Hikes: Dark Hollow Falls, Bearfence Mountain.
What I Saw: Mountains, Dark Hollow Falls, Stars.
What I Did: Hiking, ate at park restaurant, became a Junior Ranger.

Congaree National Park

Dates Visited: January 2017
Animals Seen: White-tailed deer, squirrels, red-shouldered hawk, woodpecker.
Hikes: The Boardwalk Trail.
What I Saw: Trees, Weston Lake, Mosquito Meter, Visitor Center.
What I Did: Hiking, became a Junior Ranger.

Theodore Roosevelt National Park

Dates Visited: April 2017

Animals Seen: Bison, elk, deer, wild horses, jackrabbit, longhorn steer, prarie dogs, magpies, woodpeckers.

Hikes: Oxbow Bend Overlook, North Dakota Badlands Overlook, Wind Canyon Trail, Buck Hill Trail.

What I Saw: Badlands, Maltese Cross Cabin, Little Missouri River.

What I Did: Hiking, took Scenic Loop Drive, became a Junior Ranger.

Glacier and Waterton Lakes International Peace Park

Dates Visited: April 2017

Animals Seen: Moose, Grizzly Bears, Deer.

Hikes: None

What I Saw: Waterfalls, St. Mary Lake, Lake McDonald, Lower Waterton Lake, Glaciers, Mountains.

What I Did: Plane ride, snowmobile tour, took Going-to-the-Sun Road.

North Cascades National Park

Dates Visited: April 2017

Animals Seen: Roosevelt elk.

Hikes: River Loop Trail, Trail of the Cedars.

What I Saw: Waterfalls, Newhalem Dam, trees, suspension bridge.

What I Did: Hiking, took scenic drive, became a junior ranger.

Best Trip

Day 1: We arrived in Chicago.

Day 2: We went to Medieval Times and got an R.V. One actor at MT talked to me.

Day 3: We visited Badlands Nat. Park. We saw a pronghorn. I earned a Junior Ranger badge. I also earned one at Munteman Missle. We climbed mountains.

Day 4: We visited Mount Rushmore. We walked a trail. I earned another badge. Then, we tried to put a puzzle together. We had dinner at a great place. Afterward, we saw a rodeo. Horses tried to shake off riders. Riders lassoed calfs. The kids got to chase cows. We found bunnies.

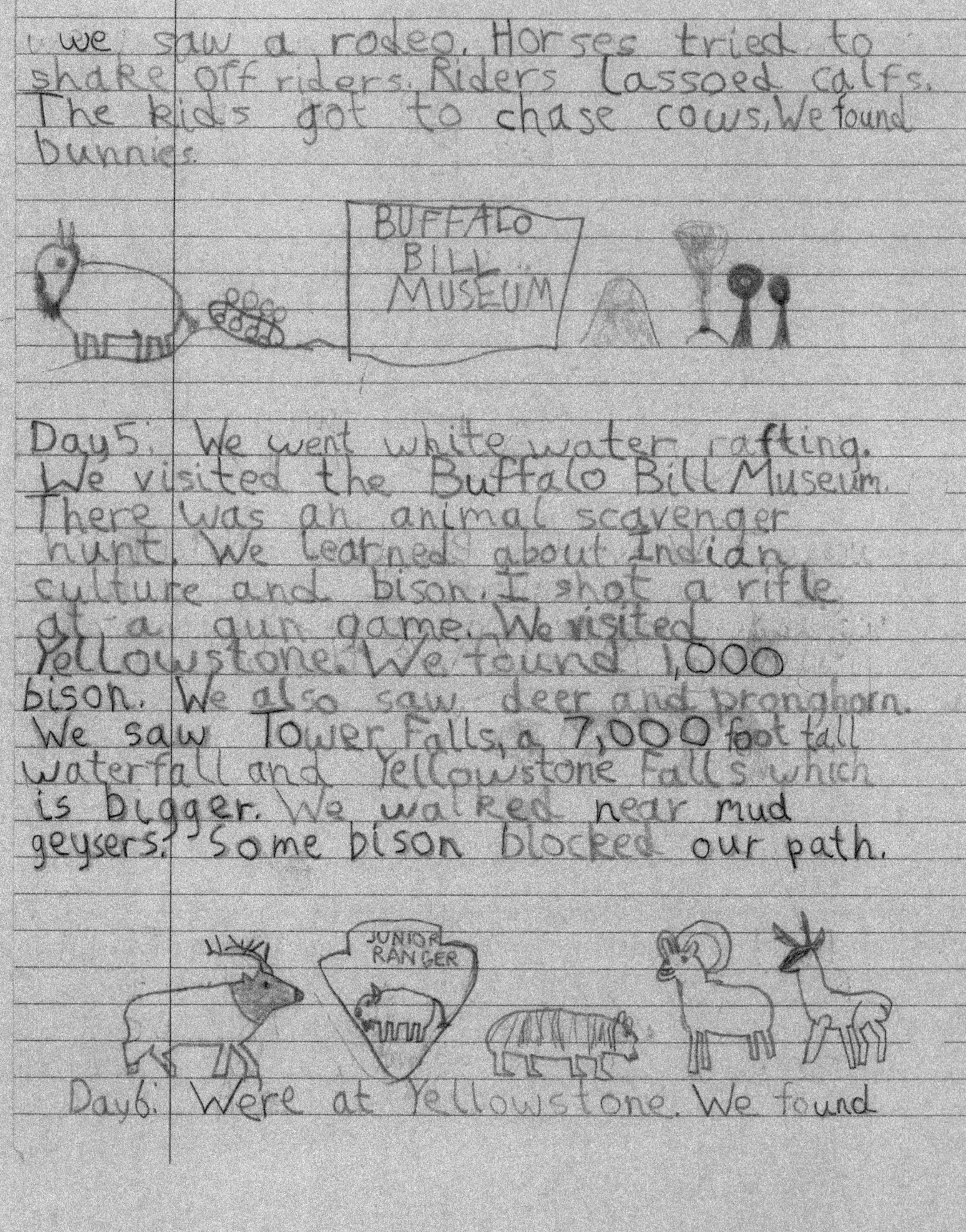

Day 5: We went white water rafting. We visited the Buffalo Bill Museum. There was an animal scavenger hunt. We learned about Indian culture and bison. I shot a rifle at a gun game. We visited Yellowstone. We found 1,000 bison. We also saw deer and pronghorn. We saw Tower Falls, a 7,000 foot tall waterfall and Yellowstone Falls which is bigger. We walked near mud geysers. Some bison blocked our path.

Day 6: We're at Yellowstone. We found

bison, elk, grizzly bear, black bear, black bear cubs, bighorn sheep, and pronghorn antelope. We saw Petrified Tree. We visited Mammoth Hot Springs. We climbed 400 ft. to the top. We explored Norris Geyser Baisin. There were many geysers including Steamboat Geyser. Steamboat was huge. I got two more ranger badges.

We saw Old Faithful. It went 60 ft. up. We walked around many geysers. We found a prarie dog.

Yellowstone Facts: There are a few dozen bighorns in the park. You will walk under a black bear three times in your life. You should fight a black bear. At the park, you're always at least 5,000 feet up. There are black grizzlies

Day 7: We SOB left CRY Yellowstone today. We visited an atomic power plant. We learned about technology. We grabbed things with a robot arm. We explored Craters of the Moon National Monument. We climbed two miles up. We went into a dark, rocky, and unauthorized cave. We were chased by hitchhikers. We went to Boise and saw the capital building.

DAY8. We visited Reno Nevada. They had some casinos. We saw Carson City, the capital of Nevada. The building was great. I got a new hat. We went to a gas station. The "S" was gone in Shell. We got ice cream. We arrived at Yosemite. There was a coyote and some deer.

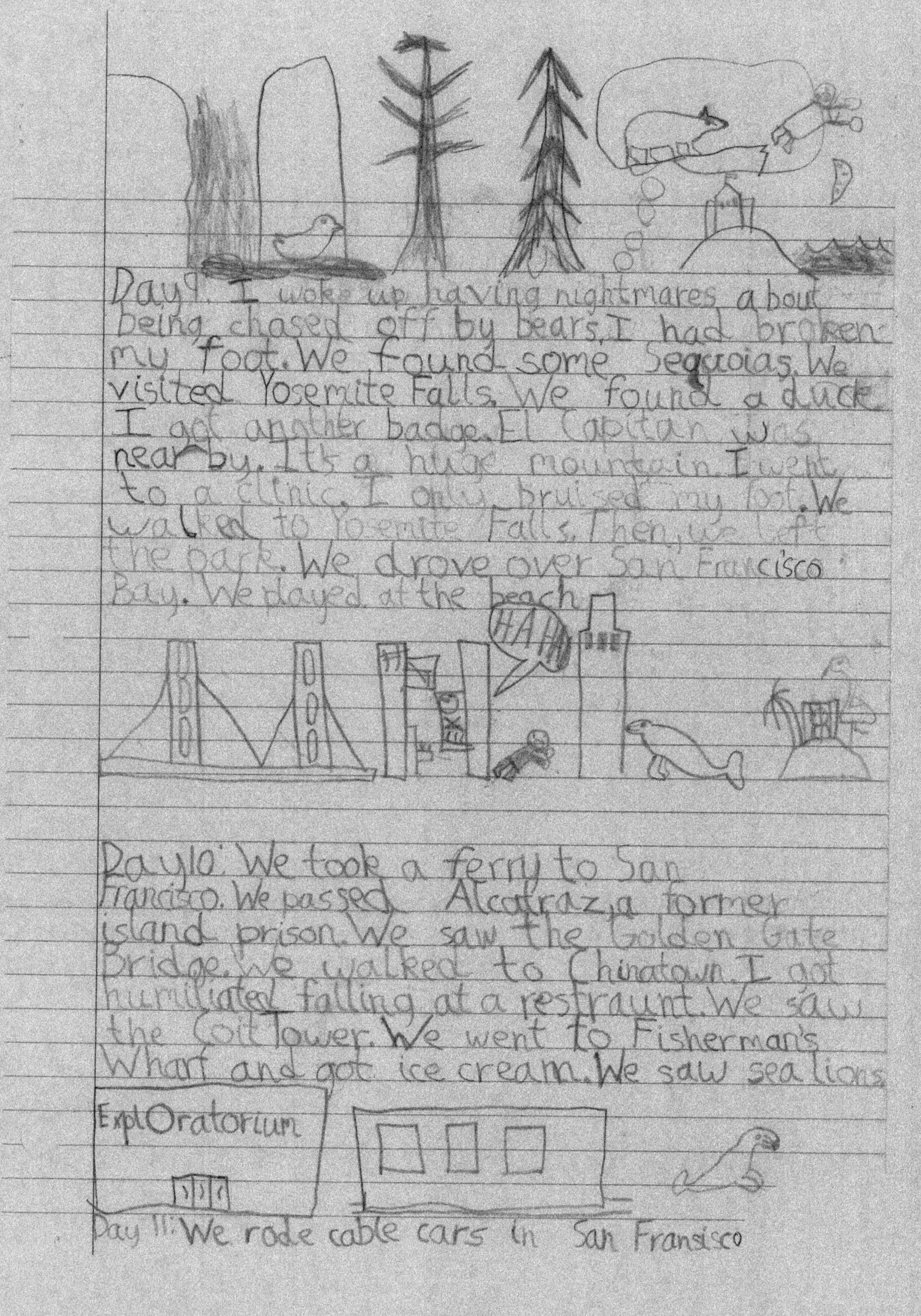

Day 9: I woke up having nightmares about being chased off by bears. I had broken my foot. We found some Sequoias. We visited Yosemite Falls. We found a duck. I got another badge. El Capitan was nearby. It's a huge mountain. I went to a clinic. I only bruised my foot. We walked to Yosemite Falls. Then, we left the park. We drove over San Francisco Bay. We played at the beach.

Day 10: We took a ferry to San Francisco. We passed Alcatraz, a former island prison. We saw the Golden Gate Bridge. We walked to Chinatown. I got humiliated falling at a restraunt. We saw the Coit Tower. We went to Fisherman's Wharf and got ice cream. We saw sea lions.

Day 11: We rode cable cars in San Fransisco

We visited an aquarium. I touched a shark.
We saw sea lions again. We found the
ExplOratorium. I got squirted by a drink
fountain. I made an animation. We had
dinner.

There were many places we
went to. This was the best trip!
TOP 10

1. Yellowstone
2. San Fransisco
3. Yosemite
4. Mount Rushmore
5. Craters of the Moon
6. Badlands
7. Carson City Capital
8. Boise Capital
9. Madison Capital
10. Minuteman Missle
11. The RV

The Good, The Badlands, and the Awesome

Friday, April 7th, 2017: Once I arrived in Chicago on a plane, my family and I drove to Indiana. We picked up an RV and headed to Minneapolis.

Saturday, April 8th, 2017: My dad drove us to Minnehaha Falls, a decently-sized waterfall. After that, we headed to the Mall of America. My brother and I rode SpongeBob Rock Bottom Plunge at Nick Universe. Afterwards, we journeyed on to Theodore Roosevelt National Park. We arrived at dusk, which is a good time to look for wildlife. We saw elk, bison, wild horses, deer, and squirrels.

Sunday, April 9th, 2017: I am still in Theodore Roosevelt National Park. I am in Cottonwood Campground in the South Unit. My sister and I followed animal tracks and scat to the Missouri River. We found wild horses. Later, the whole family took the Scenic Loop Drive. We saw many bison, prarie dogs, and mule deer. We also saw some woodpeckers. My mom, brother, and I hiked Wind Canyon Trail. We saw a jackrabbit. We also saw geese at Buck Hill Trail. Next, we all headed to the North Unit. Before reaching Oxbow Bend Overlook, We saw bison and longhorn steer. After viewing the park, we drove to Fort Union Historic Site. We saw old artifacts from times after the Civil War.

Monday, April 10th, 2017. We arrived at the border of the United States and Canada. We drove to Waterton Lakes National Park. We saw waterfalls, frozen waterfalls, glaciers, and crystal blue lakes. Ducks and geese were flying over the lakes and mountains. Once we made it back to the United States, we drove to Glacier National Park. We drove on part of Going-to-the-Sun Road. I found a moose, which I had never seen before. I also had experiences with pronghorn antelope, prarie dogs, wild horses, and deer. We stopped at Lake McDonald.

Tuesday, April 11th, 2017. We left Glacier National Park. We saw some deer on the way out. My mom, dad, two brothers and I went on a scenic airplane flight. We saw glaciers, mountains, and incredible landscapes. Then I rode a snowmobile and saw huge mountains. I also saw a grizzly bear. After that, we drove to Big Arm State Park.

Wednesday, April 12th, 2017: We went to the National Bison Range. We saw bison, deer, antelope, magpies and Canada geese. Later, we visited Turnbull National Wildlife Refuge. We saw geese, ducks, and meadowlarks. Then we reached our campground. We saw Roosevelt elk and mule deer.

Thursday, April 13th, 2017: We saw more elk at our campground this morning. Next, we took a hike through a temperate rainforest. Then, we drove to Seattle. We had New England clam chowder at Pike Place Chowder. We also had cheese at Beecher's Cheese Factory. We also had donuts, croissants, and grilled cheese. We saw bald eagles overhead. We also visited Snoqualmie Falls with rainbows nearby. Later, we got a tour of the Boeing Factory. We saw 747s in the world's largest building. We also saw planes (787s) that don't exist yet get built. Afterwards, we saw porpoises on a ferry ride. We rode the ferry to Fort Casey State Park. We saw lighthouses, cannons, elk, deer, and rabbits.

The Last Frontier

Monday, July 16, 2018: This morning, we all took a van to RSW. We saw soft shell turtles and key deer. We flew to Atlanta. We boarded a plane there and flew to Anchorage. During the flight, we flew over North Dakota and saw The Badlands. We saw mountains, glaciers, and lakes as we flew over Alaska. Before landing, we saw a female moose and her calf near a lake. Next, we drove to Sheep Mountain Lodge. We saw trees, mountains, glaciers and rivers. At the lodge, we found a bunny and went to sleep afterwards.

Tuesday, July 17, 2018: This morning, we took a quick trip to Matanuska Glacier. We saw two moose and some hares. Next, we ate breakfast at our lodge. I liked the salmon omelette and sour dough pancakes. After breakfast, we drove to Wrangell-St. Elias National Park. We saw woodpeckers, magpies and squirrels. The trees and mountains were beautiful. The kids all became Junior Rangers before leaving. We drove on Denali Highway. We saw many mountains, glaciers and lakes. We saw a wolf and some ground squirrels. A few hours later, we arrived at Denali National Park. We checked in at McKinley Creekside Cabins and entered the park. We saw three moose, a beaver, his dam and hiked Horseshoe Lake Trail.

Wednesday, July 18, 2018: We all woke up early and had breakfast. I ate french toast pancakes. Afterwards, we drove into the park. We boarded a bus when we arrived. This bus took us on the 8-hour Tundra Wilderness tour. The tour took us to mountains, rivers, valleys, glaciers, and icefields. There were no clouds in the sky, so we could clearly see Denali. At the place where we first saw Denali, we also saw a moose. Then, we saw a fox walking along the road and two more foxes playing in the meadow. The next animals we saw were three grizzly bears on a hill. We also saw two caribou cross the road. Then we saw willow ptarmigins, arctic ground squirrels and snowshoe hares. After that, we saw a glacier and two dozen caribou climbing a mountain. Then, we found another bear and two cubs. We went to a rest stop where we saw four Dall's sheep on top of a mountain. Later, we reached the final stop before we turned around. We got stunning views of Denali and other mountains in the area. Then, we turned around. On the way back, we saw five grizzly bears and four cubs. We also saw the Dall's sheep and a caribou running on the road. After the bus tour, we became Junior Rangers. Then, we hiked the Savage River Loop Trail. We saw a moose after the hike. We all had an early dinner that evening. Then we went back to our cabins. Tyler, Daddy and I left a little later. We went whitewater rafting with Denali Raft Adventures. The rapids were very intense and I got to go into the Nenana River. On our way back to the cabin, we saw a female moose and her calf.

Thursday, July 19, 2018: This morning, we left the cabins and drove to Anchorage. On the way, we saw Denali many times. In Anchorage, we got a new rental car and drove to Seward from there. We went to Kenai Fjords National Park when we got to Seward. We visited the Exit Glacier Nature Center and hiked to Exit Glacier. The glacier was beautiful and had a river going through it. Then, the youngest three kids became Junior Rangers. Afterwards, we ate dinner in Seward. We saw a bald eagle on the way there. I had clam chowder and grilled cheese for dinner. After dinner, we drove to our cabin that we would sleep in. The cabin was at Miller's Landing. We saw golden eagles and went to the beach outside of the cabin. Then, we went to

Friday, July 20, 2018: This morning, we went to the Kenai Fjords Visitor Center. I turned in my Explorer's Journal and earned a pin. Then, we walked along Seward's pier and saw a sea otter. We then boarded the Radiance of the Seas, a Royal Caribbean cruise ship. We enjoyed the ship's amenities for a few hours. Later, we had dinner in the Cascades Dining Room. The ship departed afterwards. I saw a humpback whale as we left. Then, I went to bed so I could prepare for the adventure that was just beginning.

Saturday, July 21, 2018: For most of the day, I enjoyed the ship's amenities. We did not go to any port today, but we did visit Hubbard Glacier. Hubbard Glacier in Wrangell-St. Elias National Park. We saw icebergs, waterfalls, Mount St. Elias, other mountains, and the calving glacier. I spent hours marveling at the glacier. Eventually, the ship left the area. We had dinner and went to bed afterwards.

Sunday, July 22, 2018: This morning, the ship arrived in Juneau. We left the boat and walked to the State Capitol Building. On the way back to the ship, we saw a black bear, bald eagles, and a river with hundreds of salmon. Later, we boarded a helicopter and flew to a dog sled camp. We saw mountains, glaciers, and waterfalls from the helicopter. The dog sled camp was situated on Mendenhall Glacier and is surrounded by mountains. When we arrived, we boarded a sled and took a ride. Afterwards, we boarded a helicopter and landed on a different part of Mendenhall Glacier. It was the most beautiful place I've ever been to. The glacier was surrounded by waterfalls and mountains. The glacier itself had colorful ice shaped in unique ways, blue ice and white snow that I walked on, deep lakes and shallow streams of the purest blue with the purest drinking water, transparent ice, and a waterfall that pours into a hole in the glacier, the likes of which you've never seen. After this, we flew back to

Juneau. We boarded the ship and prepared for departure. I wish we could have stayed longer.

Monday, July 23, 2018: Today, our cruise ship docked in Skagway. Skagway is a city inside the Klondike Gold Rush National Historic Site. We visited the historic site's visitor center and became Junior Rangers. Later, we boarded a bus that took us to Yukon Territory. On the bus, we saw mountains, lakes, rivers, forests, glaciers, forests, and waterfalls. We eventually arrived at the Yukon border. As we turned around, we saw a black bear. We returned to Skagway a few hours later. Then, the boat set sail for Icy Strait Point.

Tuesday, July 24, 2018: The cruise ship docked at Icy Strait Point this morning. We took a whale watching tour with Hoonah Bay Adventures. We saw many humpback whales, orcas, sea otters, and a sea lion. Then, we boarded the boat and left Icy Strait Point. We saw orcas from the ship. For dinner, we had wear nice clothes. I had Baked Alaska for dessert.

Wednesday, July 25, 2018: Today, we visited Ketchikan. We all went fishing in the open ocean with a guide. I caught two rockfish and Lachlan caught the largest rockfish. After a few hours, we went to a camp where the fish we caught were cooked and served to us. The fish tasted very good and we had bread pudding for desert. On the way back to the port, we saw some bald eagles. Then, we left Ketchikan.

Thursday, July 26, 2018: Today, we spent the whole day on the cruise ship.

Friday, July 27, 2018: The ship docked in Vancouver as the final destination. We left the ship and went to our hotel. Next, we drove to Capilano Suspension Bridge Park. The bridge was wonderful and went over a river. We hiked many forest trails. We saw natural cliffs, trout ponds, and a great blue heron. Some people had domesticated falcons and great-horned owls. We also completed a scavenger hunt and earned a badge. Afterwards, we did the Cliffwalk, a walkway that sticks out of a cliff. Then, we walked to Stanley Park and visited the Vancouver Aquarium. We saw, fish, sharks, scarlet ibises, a sloth, macaws, jellyfish, sea lions, seals, sea otters, a dolphin, walruses, stingrays, turtles, alligators, and many other animals. After that, we walked around Stanley Park. We saw a sea lion, herons, cormorants, Canada geese, and Lumberjack Arch. We had dinner at an Oyster Bar that night.

Saturday, July 28, 2018: This morning, we took an Aquabus to Granville Island. Granville Island has shopping and a farmer's market. Then, we visited a museum called Scienceworld. Exhibits were about the human body, innovation, animals, illusions, and materials. Next, we went to a train station. We all boarded a train that took us to Seattle. When we got to Seattle, we went our hotel and went to sleep.

Sunday, July 29, 2018: This morning, we went to Pike Place Market. We enjoyed cheese at Beecher's and clam chowder at Pike Place Chowder House. Next, we walked around Seattle. Emily, Lachlan, and Daddy saw a soccer game. The rest of us saw a playground, walked to Amazon's Headquarters, and went to the top of the Space Needle. Then, we all boarded a plane.

Monday, July 30, 2018: We arrived in Detroit this morning before flying home. We got home a few hours later. I'll miss Alaska, but who knows where I might go next.

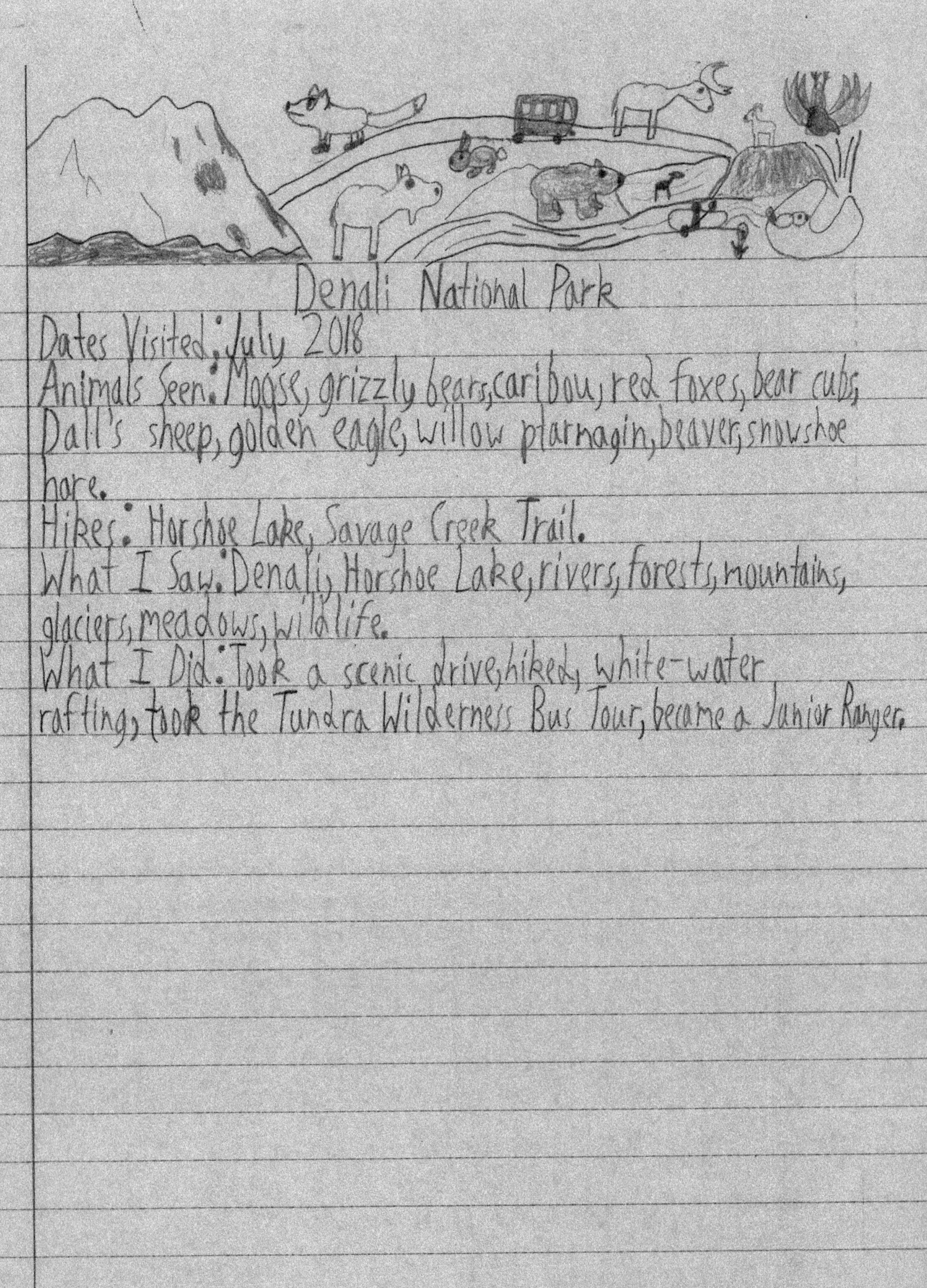

Denali National Park

Dates Visited: July 2018
Animals Seen: Moose, grizzly bears, caribou, red foxes, bear cubs, Dall's sheep, golden eagle, willow ptarmagin, beaver, snowshoe hare.
Hikes: Horshoe Lake, Savage Creek Trail.
What I Saw: Denali, Horshoe Lake, rivers, forests, mountains, glaciers, meadows, wildlife.
What I Did: Took a scenic drive, hiked, white-water rafting, took the Tundra Wilderness Bus Tour, became a Junior Ranger.

Pleasures in the Desert

A Trip to 8 Southern National Parks

Tuesday, June 9th, 2020: Before the trip, we did some normal stuff. However, it wasn't long before Daddy arrived home from Miami with an RV. I drove in the RV for a brief period and did a pretty good job. We took a long drive to Paynes Prairie State Park in Micanopy where we would spend the night. When we arrived, we saw many deer frolicking. We drove to the visitor center to do a hike. The trail went to the Wacahoota Observation Tower. From the top, we saw six deer and over 30 bison in the distance. Afterwards, we saw a large lizard. We then drove to Puc Puggy Campground, our accomadations for the night. The camp had many lush forests that contrasted the vast prairie. When we parked, Tyler, Daddy, and I walked to Lake Wauberg and watched the sunset. Overall, Paynes Prairie is a great state park and a must-see if you're near Gainesville.

Wednesday, June 10th, 2020: This morning, we returned to the Observation Tower. We saw spiders and caterpillars on the trail and deer and wild horses from the tower. We also found sandhill cranes. As we left, we found a boardwalk where we saw fish, a gator, kestrels, and limpkins. At this point, we began a long drive to Mississippi. We ate Bojangles chicken and biscuits for lunch. On the drive, we saw a deer, a tortoise, and a coyote. We stopped at the Alabama Capitol in Montgomery. In the evening, we reached a forested campground called Whitten Park where we spent the night.

Thursday, June 11th, 2020: We embarked on a drive to our first national park of the trip, Hot Springs. We stopped in Memphis and saw Mud Island and a large Bass Pro Shop. After more driving, we reached Little Rock. We got takeout from Gus's Fried Chicken. The chicken, macaroni, and fries were all delicious. After seeing the state capitol, we drove to Hot Springs National Park. We passed Magic Springs Theme park and some wild turkeys on the way in. We started at Gulpha Gorge Campground with forests, a creek, and insects like butterflies and dragonflies. We reserved a spot and drove to Bathhouse Row. We found a display spring and hiked Grand Promenade. The quiet trail had bees, plants, and views of Bathhouse Row. After that, we walked in front of the baths and became Junior Rangers. Then, we took the Hot Springs Mountain Drive. We stopped at the mountain and saw a view from a pavillion. Then, we hiked Hot Springs Mountain. We saw a cardinal and a salamander. After a stop at Happy Hollow Spring for water, we went to Balanced Rock. We saw two deer and a mammal I thought was a fox. The trail was nice and the rocks were large. Afterwards, we returned to Gulpha Gorge. Tyler, Mommy, and I hiked to Goat Rock from the campground. We saw two robins and crossed the creek on rocks. Goat Rock gave us a pleasant view of the Ouachita Mountains. We turned in for the night. Overall, I was pleasantly surprised by the park. While the scenery was average and the town was awful, the quiet hikes and wildlife were enjoyable. I also liked the architecture and campground. What I expected to be the worst park ended up being okay. It's not amazing, but it's fun. While not truly deserving of park status, it sits comfortably between good and bad parks.

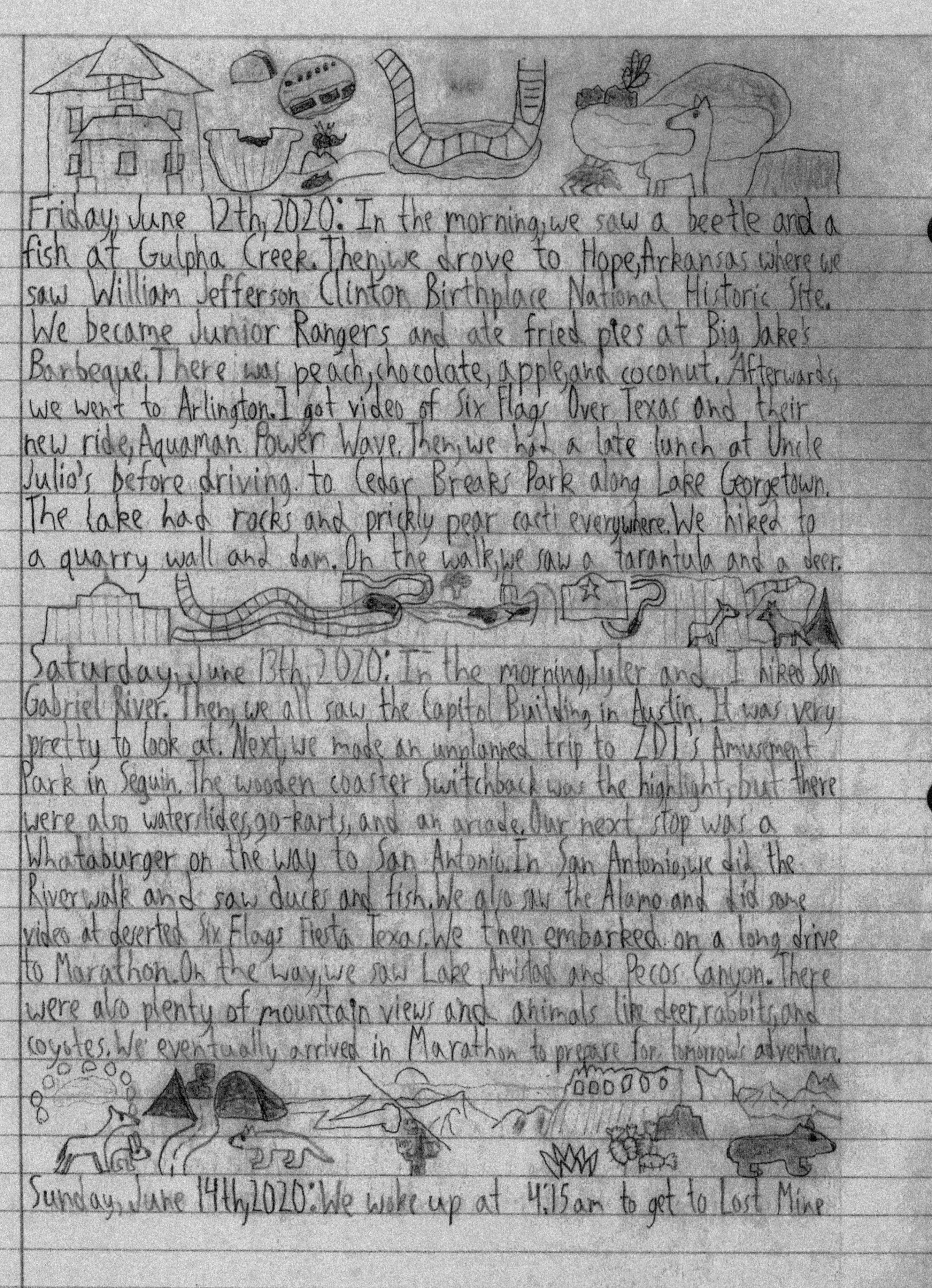

Friday, June 12th, 2020: In the morning, we saw a beetle and a fish at Gulpha Creek. Then, we drove to Hope, Arkansas where we saw William Jefferson Clinton Birthplace National Historic Site. We became Junior Rangers and ate fried pies at Big Jake's Barbeque. There was peach, chocolate, apple, and coconut. Afterwards, we went to Arlington. I got video of Six Flags Over Texas and their new ride, Aquaman Power Wave. Then, we had a late lunch at Uncle Julio's before driving to Cedar Breaks Park along Lake Georgetown. The lake had rocks and prickly pear cacti everywhere. We hiked to a quarry wall and dam. On the walk, we saw a tarantula and a deer.

Saturday, June 13th, 2020: In the morning, Tyler and I hiked San Gabriel River. Then, we all saw the Capitol Building in Austin. It was very pretty to look at. Next, we made an unplanned trip to ZDT's Amusement Park in Seguin. The wooden coaster Switchback was the highlight, but there were also water slides, go-karts, and an arcade. Our next stop was a Whataburger on the way to San Antonio. In San Antonio, we did the Riverwalk and saw ducks and fish. We also saw the Alamo and did some video at deserted Six Flags Fiesta Texas. We then embarked on a long drive to Marathon. On the way, we saw Lake Amistad and Pecos Canyon. There were also plenty of mountain views and animals like deer, rabbits, and coyotes. We eventually arrived in Marathon to prepare for tomorrow's adventure.

Sunday, June 14th, 2020: We woke up at 4:15 am to get to Lost Mine

Trail before the only RV spot was taken. Before leaving we stepped outside to see a sky full of stars and the Milky Way. As we drove, we saw many deer, jackrabbits, and a coyote. Upon entering, we saw many cacti like prickly pear and century plant (aloe). As we approached the Chisos Mountains, the orange and yellow sunrise framed the peaks. When we arrived at the trail, we were alone. Daddy, Tyler, and I began the hike. The mountains were lit up by the morning light. On the hike, we passed many cacti, flowers, and birds. The views along the were dramatic and beautiful, but the final view atop Lost Mine Peak was the best as the mountains and Rio Grande in the distance and the sun peaking out from a mountain. At the end of the trail, there was a rock that went even higher. As we climbed the rock, we saw a black bear on the trail where we had been minutes ago. We watched him as he walked up and down the mountainside, scratching himself and eating. After fifteen minutes, the bear left and we headed back to the trailhead. Our next stop was the Panther Junction Visitor Center. The facilities were closed, but the Panther Path was not. This short walk gave me nice mountain views and went past many healthy prickly pears and other desert plants. I saw a jackrabbit and a four-lined skink. Later, we arrived at a tunnel that was headed for the Rio Grande and Sierra Del Carmen. We saw a squirrel and smaller rodent on the way. Soon, we arrived at the Rio Grande Village Nature Trail. The trail had a plethora of wildlife. I saw tons of birds, but my favorites were zone-tailed hawks, greater roadrunners, and a vermillion flycatcher. We also saw lizards, rabbits, fish, dragonflies, and many locusts. Afterwards, we went to Boquillas Canyon Trail and saw the Border Crossing. The canyon was tall, beautiful, and had the teal Rio Grande running through. We saw some birds and lizards on the trail.

After seeing that part of the park, we drove the Ross Maxwell Scenic Drive. On the drive, we saw many colorful mountains. Our first stop on the road was Sotol Vista. The views of mountains, Santa Elena Canyon, and the Rio Grande were great. Our next stop was Mule Ears Overlook. The twin peaks were unique and picturesque. We drove to Tuff Canyon, next. The walls were deep and white. After driving by mountains, arches, and even a wild horse, we arrived at Santa Elena Canyon. This was our final stop and it was beautiful. The massive canyon was carved by the Rio Grande as Terlingua Creek fed into it. Sadly, you had to cross the creek to reach the trail, which we couldn't do. After taking some photos, we began a long drive to the Organ Mountains. We stopped in El Paso and Las Cruces on the way. When we arrived at the camp, we found that it was not open. We ended up sleeping at Baylor Canyon Trail. We saw a rabbit and a horned lizard before we fell asleep. The sunset was great.

Monday, June 15th, 2020: This morning, we saw two antelope jackrabbits at the trailhead. Afterward, we left to White Sands National Park. The park was closed, but we pulled over at a place where could see the beautiful, untouched dunes with mountains in the background. Next, we drove to Tombstone, Arizona. The old western town was very authentic. We watched a reenactment of Wyatt Earp's shootout at the O.K. Corral. We also collected The Tombstone Epitaph from the day of the shootout. Soon, we arrived at Saguaro National Park. In the park, we saw thousands of saguaro cacti. Today, we explored the park's eastern unit. The Cactus Forest Drive was short and twisty as it took us to overlooks of desert plants and mountains, including

Rincon Peak. We saw many birds such as gila woodpeckers, white-winged doves, and cactus wrens. Our first trail was Desert Ecology. We saw many cacti up close. We also found a raptor called a ferruginious hawk. As we continued driving, we saw an ornate tree lizard. We stopped at some views and soon reached Javelina Rocks. The formations were cool and we saw some birds. We eventually reached Freeman Homestead Trail. The home is long gone, but there was plenty of wildlife. We found small birds, lizards, and rabbits. As we reached some cliffs, some large birds started flying around. I used binoculars to find out they were great-horned owls. After the trail, we drove into In 'N' Out Burger and I ate a delicious Double Double. Soon, we were in Gilbert Ray Campground which had many cacti. We decided to watch a sunset at Gates Pass Overlook. The vibrant colors were beautiful and I found two eastern collared lizards. That night, I took photos of stars and cacti that came out very well.

Tuesday, June 16th, 2020. We woke up early and saw rabbits, an antelope ground squirrel, and a quail. As we entered the western part of Saguaro National Park, we saw a coyote. As we arrived, we saw even more cacti than the previous day. Our first trail left from the visitor center and was called Cactus Garden. You walk through Javelina Wash to see desert plants. We saw many cacti and rabbits. Next, we hiked the Desert Discovery Nature Trail. On the trail, there were many cacti, lizards, and rabbits. After that, we hiked the Valley View Overlook Trail. On the trail, we saw many lizards including chuckwalla. The final view had too many saguaros to count and plenty of birds and lizards.

We saw even more lizards on our way back to the RV. Our final hike was Signal Hill. At the trailhead, I found a large, spiny lizard. The trail climbed up a hill to some petroglyphs. On top, I found a squirrel and a kangaroo rat. Afterwords, we returned to the visitor center and earned Junior Ranger badges. We saw another quail and even a golden eagle on top of a saguaro. Afterwards, we toured the Arizona-Sonora Desert Museum. The museum had a few exhibits about rocks and fossils, but the animals were the best. The exhibits had every desert animal you could imagine and more. My favorites were black bears, mountain lions, gray foxes, javelinas, and the aviary birds. The surrounding area was Saguaro National Park, which made the animals feel more wild. There were even some wild birds and lizards. Afterwards, we took a long drive to Petrified Forest National Park. The drive took us through a beautiful canyon. We reached Petrified Forest at 4:00pm, but the park closed at 5:00pm. This meant we had to hurry. Our first stop was Crystal Forest. Many petrified logs had colorful crystals inside of them. Along the way, we saw many geological formations of white and yellow. We thought we saw some, but they were far away. Our next stop was Blue Mesa. The large badland formations were blue, purple, and gray. They were massive and uniquely shaped. I personally liked this hike the most. We finished hiking after closing, so we had to leave. On the way out, we stopped at overlooks of the Painted Desert. The sky had smoke, but the reds and oranges still looked amazing. Afterwards, we drove to Grand Canyon National Park. We saw a deer near the Trailer Village where we would spend the night. Once we set up camp for the night, we went outside to stargaze. The stars were abundant, bright, and beautiful. This was great stargazing in our third national park of the day.

Wednesday, June 17th, 2020: This morning, we woke up in the south rim and headed to Bright Angel Trail. We saw many elk on the way, including some calves. Soon, I began a six-mile hike to Plateau Point with Mommy and Tyler. Not far up the trail, I found an endangered California condor. As we continued the hike, we ended up over 3,000 feet below the rim and saw the rock formations change around us. We saw squirrels, chipmunks, and lizards. As we reached Indian Garden, we ate lunch under trees. We met some rangers who gave us a special Phantom Ranch Junior Ranger Booklet. Afterwards, we hiked another 1.5 miles to Plateau Point. This portion of the trail was surrounded by canyon walls and the view of the green, rushing Colorado River was unmatched. As we returned to Indian Garden, I dipped my feet in Bright Angel Creek to quickly refresh. Afterwards, Tyler and I earned badges, patches, and stickers for our booklet. We then began our hike back up the canyon. It had gotten very hot, so the hike was grueling. When we reached the 1.5-mile resthouse, Daddy was waiting with extra drinks. He found a deer behind the house. Soon, we reached the top of the rim. After a long break, we traveled to a couple of overlooks along the south rim. At Navajo and Lipan Point, we enjoyed views of the canyon and blue Colorado River. For sunset, we went to Moran Point and watched colors fill the canyon. Finally, we went to Mather Point for stargazing. As we returned to the camp, I found deer.

Thursday, June 18th, 2020: This morning, we found many elk outside our campsite. Before leaving Grand Canyon, we went to Maricopa Point. Next, we began a drive to Page, Arizona. On the way, we went to Sunset Crater Volcano Monument. We hiked A'a Trail where we saw lava flows, mountains, and a lizard that was black. We also earned Junior Ranger badges. Next, we drove to Wupatki National Monument. We hiked around the Box Canyon and Lomaki Pueblo. The cliff dwellings were cool and we saw an eastern collared lizard up close. We also viewed Grand Canyon's north rim from above. When we arrived in Page, we ordered from Big John's Texas BBQ. The ribs, brisket, and pulled pork were great. Next, we went to Wahweap RV Park along Lake Powell. We also saw Glen Canyon Dam on the way. After checking in, we went to Horshoe Bend. We walked to the overlook and saw a lizard on the way. The overlook was amazing as we watched the sunset. There were more lizards and fantastic colors. Before going to bed, we found a bunny.

Friday, June 19th, 2020: This morning, we went to Lake Powell Marina where we got a boat to explore Glen Canyon. As we boarded, we saw many ducks and carp. Soon, we went on a fast, fun boat ride to Rainbow Bridge National Monument. On the way, we saw many rock formations of Glen Canyon and Monument Valley. After two hours, we reached Rainbow Bridge. On the hike to the arch, we found some small birds. However, the natural bridge was the highlight. It was massive and intricately shaped. As we headed back to the boat, we saw lizards crawl across the canyon walls above Lake Powell. On the way back to Wahweap, we went tubing and swimming in the lake. Soon enough, we returned to Wahweap and headed to Nevada. We took a long drive to Valley of Fire State Park. We arrived at sunset, which turned the rocks a bright orange. We saw a bunny on the way to Atlatl Rock Campground where we spent the night.

Saturday, June 20th, 2020: This morning we walked around Valley of Fire before unfortunately returning the RV in Las Vegas. On our walk, we saw two more lizards. Afterwards, we returned the RV and got a rental car to visit a few more stops. Before embarking on a long drive, we got lunch at In 'N' Out Burger, my favorite fast food restaurant. Around four hours later, we reached Great Basin National Park. At the visitor center, I found a small lizard. Soon, we began the Wheeler Peak Scenic Drive. This road climbed nearly 5,000 feet into the mountains. As we drove through mountains, we looked out to see the Great Basin Desert below. On the drive, we found some chipmunks and squirrels and stopped at Mather Overlook. Soon, we reached Bristlecone Trail. At the start of the trail, we walked over a creek. After a while, we reached Teresa Lake. The lake was small, but the colors, clarity, and views of Wheeler Peak were great. Soon enough, we reached the bristlecone pine grove. The trees were twisty and over 3,000 years old. It was cool to walk amongst such old living things. After, or as we reached Wheeler Peak Glacier which is the only one in Nevada. The glacier was large and the mountain was beautiful. As we returned to the car, we found Clark's nutcrackers and deer. We then left the park. We found a wild turkey on the way out. While driving to our next stop, we found many pronghorn antelope and hawks. The drive was long, but it was worth it. Late that night, we arrived in Springdale, Utah. We stayed in a hotel that night. This was our only night in a hotel, but we had one more park to visit.

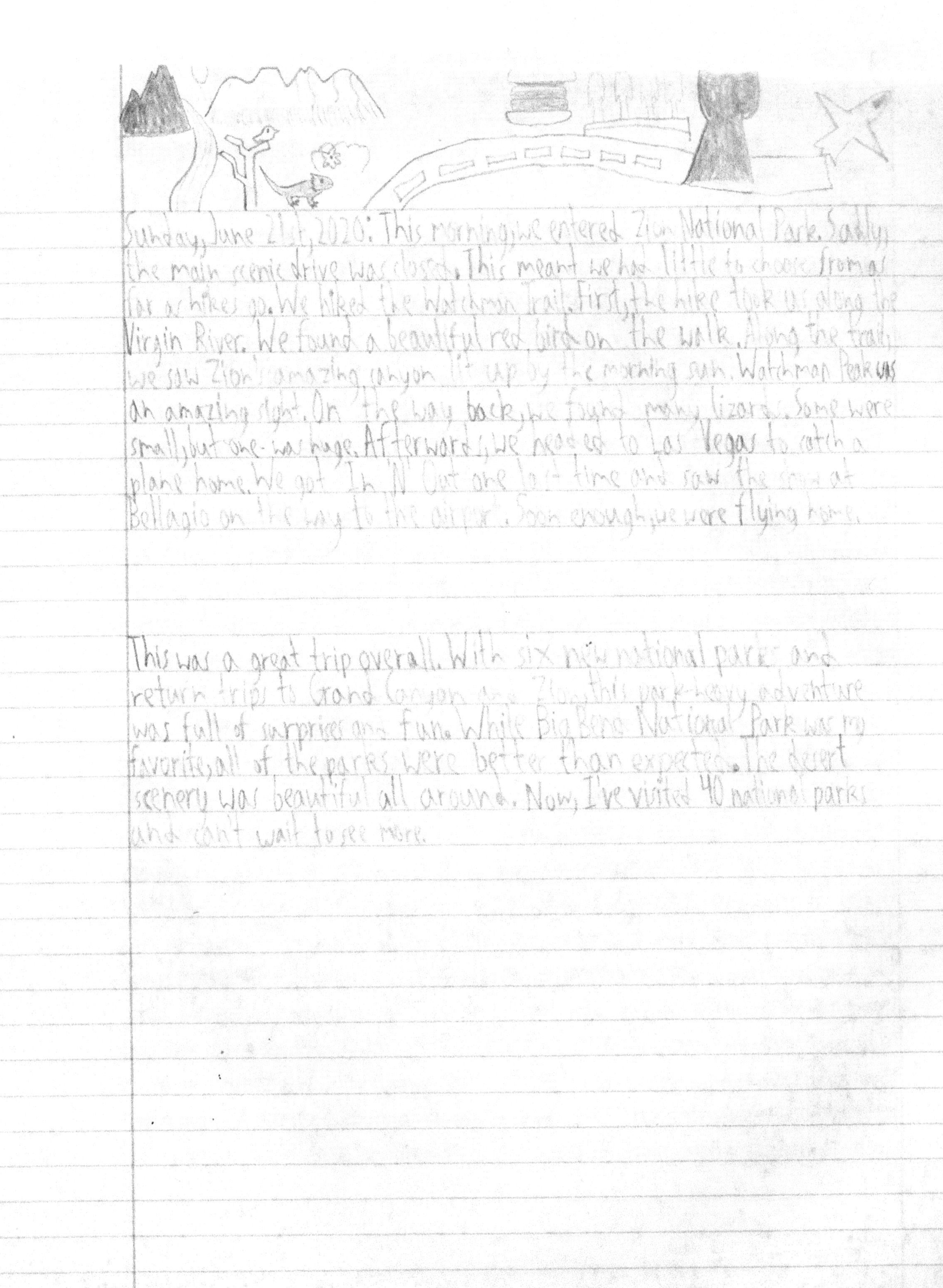

Sunday, June 21st, 2020: This morning, we entered Zion National Park. Sadly, the main scenic drive was closed. This meant we had little to choose from as far as hikes go. We hiked the Watchman Trail. First, the hike took us along the Virgin River. We found a beautiful red bird on the walk. Along the trail, we saw Zion's amazing canyon lit up by the morning sun. Watchman Peak was an amazing sight. On the way back, we found many lizards. Some were small, but one was huge. Afterwards, we headed to Las Vegas to catch a plane home. We got In 'N' Out one last time and saw the snow at Bellagio on the way to the airport. Soon enough, we were flying home.

This was a great trip overall. With six new national parks and return trips to Grand Canyon and Zion, this park-heavy adventure was full of surprises and fun. While Big Bend National Park was my favorite, all of the parks were better than expected. The desert scenery was beautiful all around. Now, I've visited 40 national parks and can't wait to see more.

Top 15 Attractions

1. Juneau (Mendenhall Glacier)
2. Denali National Park
3. Kenai Fjords National Park
4. Wrangell-St. Elias National Park
5. Icy Strait Point
6. Stanley Park
7. Matanuska Glacier
8. Skagway
9. Ketchikan
10. Denali Highway
11. Capilano Suspension Bridge Park
12. Pike Place Market
13. Granville Island
14. Scienceworld
15. Radiance of the Seas

Top 25 National Parks

1. Yellowstone
2. Denali
3. Yosemite
4. Big Bend
5. Glacier
6. Zion
7. Grand Canyon
8. Olympic
9. Theodore Roosevelt
10. Channel Islands
11. Death Valley
12. Bryce Canyon
13. Rocky Mountain
14. Mount Rainier
15. Sequoia
16. Hawaii Volcanoes
17. Haleakala
18. Arches
19. Great Basin
20. Pinnacles
21. Carlsbard Caverns
22. Saguaro
23. Kenai Fjords
24. Wrangell-St. Elias
25. Joshua Tree

An Ode to U.S. National Parks

A is for ACADIA: the only park in Maine. A also is for ARCHES with some desert-like terrain.

B is for   : home of Bryce Ampitheater. And B is for BISCAYNE which is the scuba-diving leader.

C for CHANNEL ISLANDS: home of sea lions and seals. And C for CANYONLANDS with a strange place known as the Needles.

D is for DEATH VALLEY: you should visit in November. And D for DENALI with a mountain you'll remember.

E is for EVERGLADES: a home for snakes and gators. But watch them from a distance or they might attack you later.

F is for FORT JEFFERSON: a fort in Dry Tortugas.

G for GLACIER BAY with whales like humpbacks and belugas. G also is for GLACIER: it has mountain goats and bears. G for GRAND CANYON and GRAND TETON with views everywhere.

H is for HOT SPRINGS were the water's very warm. The water starts to bubble, and it takes a gaseous form.

I for INDEPENDENCE HALL: don't ring the bell, you can't!

J is for JOSHUA TREE: it's home to yucca plants.

K is for KENAI FJORDS: home of mountain goats and whales.

L is for LAKE CLARK: it only has one hiking trail.

M for MOUNT RAINIER: the highest peak in the Cascades. M is for a park in Kentucky known as MAMMOTH CAVE.

N is for a park in Washington called NORTH CASCADES. And N for the NATIONAL PARKS found in the U.S.A.

O is for OLYMPIC, and Olympic has it all. It has mountains, beaches, rainforests, and waterfalls.

P is for PINNACLES: The newest park you'll see. No parks start with Q, so we will skip from R to P.

R is for REDWOOD: it's where squirrels and lizards creep. And R for ROCKY MOUNTAIN which has elk and bighorn sheep.

S if for SAGUARO: it's a park in Arizona. And S for the trees in SEQUOIA and SHENANDOAH.

T for THEODORE ROOSEVELT: see bison and deer. Elk, horses and prairie dogs are also found in here.

U for the UNITED STATES where all the parks will stay.

V for VIRGIN ISLANDS: you can snorkel in a bay.

W for WRANGELL- ST. ELIAS: it's quite large. And W for WIND CAVE where some caverns have been carved.

Y for YOSEMITE because no parks start with X. When it comes to waterfalls, Yosemite is the best.

Y also is for YELLOWSTONE with wildlife galore. There are geysers, lakes, mountains and waterfalls. Need I say more?

Z is for ZION with lakes and colorful peaks. To hike and see all of Zion takes up to several weeks.